NORTHERN
AND
WESTERN
ASIA

The Sea of Galilee, Israel

The World in Maps

NORTHERN AND WESTERN ASIA

Martyn Bramwell

Lerner Publications Company • Minneapolis

**First American edition published in 2000
by Lerner Publications Company**

© 2000 by Graham Beehag Books

Lerner Publications Company
A division of Lerner Publishing Group
241 First Avenue North
Minneapolis, MN 55401 U.S.A.

Website address: www.lernerbooks.com

Library of Congress Cataloging-in-Publication Data

Bramwell, Martyn.
    Northern and western Asia / by Martyn Bramwell.
        p. cm.—(The world in maps)
Includes index.
    ISBN 0-8225-2915-7 (lib. bdg. : alk. paper)
    1. Asia—Juvenile literature. 2. Middle East—Juvenile
literature. [1. Asia.] I. Title. II. Series: Bramwell, Martyn.
The world in maps.
    DS5 .B67 2000
    950—dc21   00-009946

Printed in Singapore by Tat Wei Printing Packaging Pte Ltd
Bound in the United States of America
1 2 3 4 5 6 – OS – 05 04 03 02 01 00

Picture credits
Pages 13, 26, 28, 29, 30, 31 Robert Harding

CONTENTS

NORTHERN and WESTERN ASIA

The northern and western sections of the Asian continent comprise a vast region that covers 6,800 miles of territory. This part of Asia stretches from the deserts of the **Arabian Peninsula** in the extreme southwest across the snow-covered mountains of Kyrgyzstan and Tajikistan in western central Asia. The region includes the grassy **steppes** of Asian Russia and the ancient forests of Siberia (part of Russia). In the far Russian north lies the frozen **tundra** of the Chukchi Peninsula, which is lashed by the icy waters of the Arctic Ocean and the Bering Sea.

Northern and western Asia also exhibit some of the world's most extreme climatic conditions. For example, the desert interior of Oman in the **Middle East** is one of the hottest places on earth, with temperatures often exceeding 120ºF and sometimes soaring well above 130ºF. At the other extreme lies the Central Siberian Plateau, where, far from the moderating effects of the oceans, winter temperatures average -50ºF and often plunge to -85ºF and below.

The northern and western sections of Asia are also sparsely populated. Deserts dominate the Middle Eastern countries of the west, where populations tend to congregate in the coastal regions, in the cooler highlands farther inland, and in the main river valleys. The deserts of the Middle East are largely uninhabited, except for small groups of nomadic **Bedouin.**

The landscapes of western central Asia rise from the dry grasslands bordering the Caspian Sea to the windswept **glaciers** and peaks of the Pamir Mountains and the Tian Shan (mountains). Most of the people live near the shores of the Caspian Sea or in the foothills of the mountains, where rivers provide water for homes and for irrigating fields.

The least populated parts of northern Asia are in Asian Russia. Most of the people live in mining and industrial areas near various cities—Yekaterinburg and Chelyabinsk at the southern end of the Ural Mountains, Novosibirsk and Irkutsk in southern Siberia, and Vladivostok along the coast of the Sea of Japan. The people of the far northern forests and tundra are mainly reindeer herders, trappers, and fishers.

Farmers in the more fertile areas of northern and western Asia produce a variety of grain crops, vegetables, and fruit. Some regions grow vines for wine making, while others raise mulberry trees to provide food for silkworms. Cotton and flax are important nonfood crops in some areas, and the great forests of northern Asia produce vast quantities of lumber, plywood, pulp, and paper products. Rivers are an important source of hydroelectric power.

Oil and natural gas are the principal natural resources of the Middle East— one of the world's leading oil-producing regions. Russia also has vast reserves of both oil and gas and also extensive coalfields. Northern Asia probably has more untapped reserves of minerals than any other region in the world. Miners in the Pamir Mountains, the Tian Shan, the Ural Mountains, and the upland zones of southern Siberia produce iron, copper, lead, zinc, tungsten, tin, gold, and many other minerals. These deposits feed the region's heavy industry and manufacturing centers.

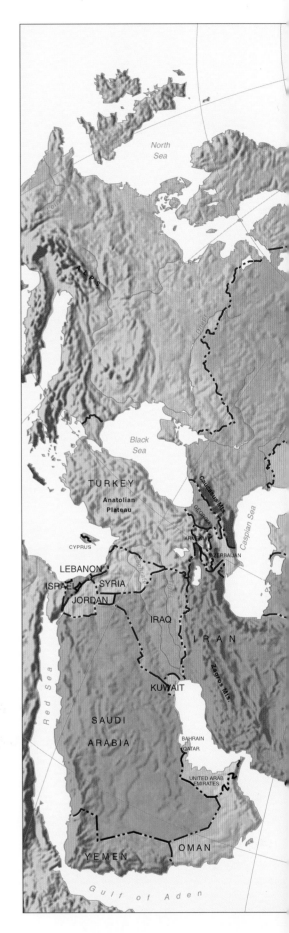

A R C T I C   O C E A N

Norwegian Sea

Barents Sea

Svalbard

0°
20°
40°
60°
80°
100°
120°
140°
160°
180°

Franz Josef Land

Novaya Zemlya

Kara Sea

Severnaya Zemlya

Laptev Sea

New Siberian Is.

East Siberian Sea

Bering Sea

Chukchi Peninsula

Kolyma Lowland

Kamchatka Peninsula

Sea of Okhotsk

Central

Siberian

Plateau

West Siberian

R   U   S   S   I   A

Plain

URAL MOUNTAINS

Plain

Ishim

Irtysh

Ob

KAZAKHSTAN

Aral Sea

Turanian Plateau

Syr Dar'ya

Balkhash

Sayan Mts.

Altai

Manchurian Plain

40°

Sea of Japan

TURKMENISTAN

UZBEKISTAN

KYRGYZSTAN

Tian Shan

TAJIKISTAN

AFGHANISTAN

Hindu Kush

Tarim Basin

Gobi Desert

Kunlan Shan

Yellow Sea

Great Basin

East China Sea

H I M A L A Y A

20°

Arabian Sea

South China Sea

0   1000   2000 Miles

0   1000   2000   3000 Km

Turkey and Cyprus

Turkey

Status:	Republic
Area:	299,158 square miles
Population:	65.9 million
Capital:	Ankara
Language:	Turkish
Currency:	Turkish lira (100 kurus)

Turkey, one of the few countries that spans continents, forms a bridge between Europe and Asia. The European portion of the country, called Thrace, comprises just 3 percent of Turkey's total landmass and sits on the southeastern tip of the continent. The remainder of the country covers a broad peninsula known as Anatolia or Asia Minor. The Straits—the Dardanelles, the Sea of Marmara, and the narrow Bosporus, all of which lead to the Black Sea—separate Turkey's two sections.

Mountain ranges along the country's northern and southern shores border Turkey's two **plateaus.** The Taurus Mountains dominate the south and almost completely hide the western plateau from the sea. The Pontic and Küre Mountains lie along the shore of the Black Sea. The country's coastal regions enjoy hot summers and mild winters, but inland Turkey is a land of extremes, with very hot, dry summers and bitterly cold winters. Less than 10 inches of rain falls each year, and parts of the land are semidesert.

Farmers on the plateaus and in the southern mountains raise sheep and goats. Those in the more fertile western valleys and northern plains grow cotton, tobacco, and olives for export and wheat, fruits, and vegetables for local markets.

Turkey's economy, long reliant on agriculture, is developing around other means of revenue. Miners in eastern Turkey excavate chromite—the country's most valuable mineral export—as well as copper, borax, and coal. Factory workers manufacture motor vehicles, chemicals, and metal, wood, and leather goods. Textiles and clothing account for about one-third of all manufactured exports. Tourism is Turkey's fastest-growing industry, enticing visitors to the historic city of Istanbul, to a wealth of ancient monuments, and to the sunny resorts along the southern coast.

Left: Ancient and modern ways of life exist side by side in rural townships like Sanliurfa in southern Turkey, near the Syrian border.

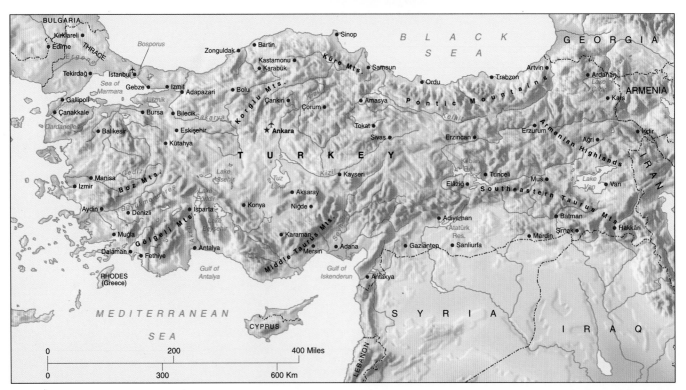

Cyprus

Status:	Republic
Area:	3,572 square miles
Population:	0.9 million
Capital:	Nicosia
Languages:	Greek, Turkish
Currency:	Cypriot pound (100 cents)
	Turkish lira (100 cents)

A small island in the eastern Mediterranean Sea, Cyprus has been divided since 1974, when Turkish forces took command of the island's northern section. The intervening years have been harsh, and the relatively poor inhabitants of the Turkish sector rely heavily on aid from Turkey. Cypriots of Greek origin remain in control of the more prosperous south, where the economy thrives despite the conflict. Repeated United Nations (UN) efforts have failed to bring about a settlement, although an uneasy standoff has replaced the bitter fighting. Only Turkey recognizes the northern section as a separate country.

Cyprus is a scenic land with a pleasant climate. Mount Olympus, the highest peak, rises to 6,403 feet in the center of the Troodos Mountains, which dominate central and western Cyprus, while the rugged limestone mountains of Kyrenia parallel the northern coast. The broad fertile Mesaoria Plain lies between the two ranges, spanning the country from Morphou in the west to Famagusta in the east.

Farmers in the north raise sheep and grow grains, grapes, olives, vegetables, and citrus fruits. Southern farmers benefit from better soil and ample water for irrigation. Their crops include fruits, salad crops, early vegetables, and flowers for export to mainland Europe.

Above: The rocky shoreline near Paphos on the southwestern coast of Cyprus is associated with Aphrodite, the Greek goddess of love and beauty.

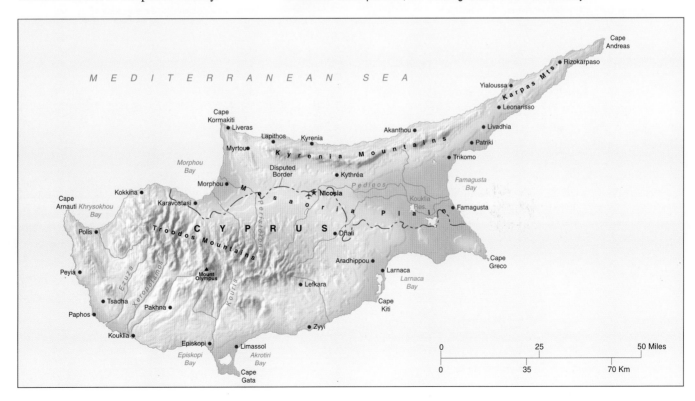

Syria

Syria

Status:	Republic
Area:	71,498 square miles
Population:	16 million
Capital:	Damascus
Languages:	Arabic, Kurdish, Armenian
Currency:	Syrian pound (100 piastres)

Syria boasts a long history and a rich culture. Some of the world's earliest farming methods developed in the fertile valleys of the Euphrates and Tigris Rivers almost 10,000 years ago. A people called the **Semites** were living in the region by about 1500 B.C. They adapted part of the Egyptian writing system to create their own alphabet. Poetry and crafts, such as weaving, glassmaking, and metalworking, flourished. More than 2,000 years ago, ancient cities such as Palmyra were important trading centers on the caravan routes linking Asia, Africa, and Europe.

Western and central Syria can be divided into three principal land regions. A narrow coastal plain along the Mediterranean Sea has rich soil and a mild, moist climate. Winds blowing in across the water provide about 40 inches of annual rain, allowing coastal farmers to grow a variety of crops without the need for irrigation. Inland from this plain and running south to the Jordanian border lie the rugged Anti-Lebanon and Jebel Druz Mountains, whose west-facing slopes catch the moisture carried by the **prevailing winds.**

To the east of the mountains lies another, less-fertile plain. Farmers here rely for irrigation on the mountain streams and the Orontes River, which flows northward through a series of gorges and broad valleys. Most Syrians live in the plains regions bordering the mountains. The capital city of Damascus, near the country's southeastern border, houses more than one million residents, and the populations in Aleppo, Homs, Hamah, and the coastal city of Latakia each exceed 150,000. Much of the remaining population live in small towns and villages that dot the countryside.

Northeast of the plains lies a vast inland plateau covered in scrub and dry grassland. Southward the land becomes more barren until it merges with the scorching sands of the Syrian Desert. The broad Euphrates River Valley winds across the plateau, providing the only fertile land in this vast, sparsely populated landscape. Farmers in scattered villages manage to grow enough food for their own needs, and small groups of nomadic Bedouin–with their camels, sheep, and goats–eke out a living in the driest desert regions.

Cotton and wheat dominate Syria's cropland, supplemented by barley, sugar beets, olives, other fruits and vegetables, and tobacco. Most farms are small family businesses and are not highly mechanized. In the poorer rural areas, many farmers still use wooden plows and hand tools to cultivate their land.

Oil wells clustered in the northeast provide Syria's chief mineral resource. Miners also extract phosphates to make fertilizer and mine gypsum and limestone for the plaster and cement used in local construction projects. Syria's chief manufacturing industries—textiles, glass, and processed foods—are concentrated in the country's large western towns.

Below: A baker in Tall Abyad in northern Syria works late into the night baking bread for the villagers' evening meal. During the Islamic month of **Ramadan,** Muslims (followers of Islam) take neither food nor drink during the hours of daylight.

Right: A Syrian woman draws water from a well in the northern city of Aleppo. This large city is a mixture of old and new. Many residents wear modern clothes and live in modern houses and apartments, but the city also has extensive older quarters with traditional houses and old marketplaces.

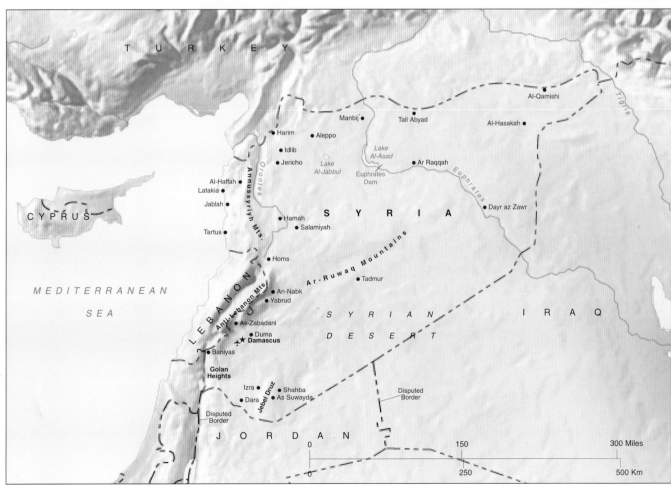

TURKEY

Al-Qamishi

Manbij
Tall Abyad
Al-Hasakah

Harim
Aleppo

Idlib
Jericho

Lake Al-Asad

Al-Haffah
Lake Al-Jabbul
Ar Raqqah

Orontes

Latakia
Euphrates Dam

Euphrates

Jablah

Annussyriyh Mts.

Hamah
S Y R I A

Salamiyah

Dayr az Zawr

Tartus

CYPRUS

Homs

Ar-Ruwaq Mountains

Tadmur

MEDITERRANEAN

An-Nabk

SEA

Yabrud

S Y R I A N

I R A Q

Anti-Lebanon Mts.

As-Zabadani

D E S E R T

L E B A N O N

Duma
Damascus

Baniyas

Golan Heights

Izra
Jebel Druz
Shahba

Dara
As Suwayda

Disputed Border

Disputed Border

J O R D A N

Tigris

0	150	300 Miles
0	250	500 Km

Lebanon

Lebanon

Status:	Republic
Area:	4,015 square miles
Population:	4.1 million
Capital:	Beirut
Languages:	Arabic, French, English
Currency:	Lebanese pound (100 piastres)

This small Arab country at the eastern end of the Mediterranean Sea has long sandy beaches backed by a narrow coastal plain. Beyond the plain, the land rises steeply to a double range of rugged mountains running north to south, parallel to the coast. The Lebanon Mountains form the first range, rising to 10,131 feet above sea level. The land then dips into the deep Bekáa Valley before rising again to the Anti-Lebanon Mountains on the border with Syria.

Hot dry summers, mild wet winters, and rich soil provide favorable farming conditions on the coastal plain. Winter rains falling on the Bekáa Valley support a second fertile farming region. Apples, peaches, oranges, lemons, grapes, and cherries are Lebanon's most valuable crops. Farmers also grow tobacco, potatoes, sugar beets, and many other vegetables for both local use and export. Lebanon's mountain regions once were famous for their cedar forests. Clear-cutting has left only sparse areas of coarse grasses and scrub for grazing sheep and goats. Factory workers in the capital city of Beirut and in Tripoli process foods and manufacture textiles, electrical goods, furniture, and chemicals.

From the 1820s to the 1970s, Beirut was one of the Middle East's leading commercial centers. Imports and exports passed regularly through Lebanon's ports. Trade flourished among Middle Eastern countries and trading partners on several continents. That prosperous era ended in the early 1970s, when civil war tore apart the country. Muslim and Christian communities clashed over the presence in Lebanon of members of the

Palestine Liberation Organization (PLO), which raided Israeli targets from base camps in Lebanon. Continued internal hostilities and retaliatory attacks by Israel against PLO bases in Lebanon caused widespread damage to Lebanon's cities—especially Beirut—and to the country's economy. Israel withdrew its forces from southern Lebanon in 2000. Despite the problems of the past, many of Lebanon's banks and businesses have survived, and the government is working to rebuild homes, factories, and roads damaged by the wars.

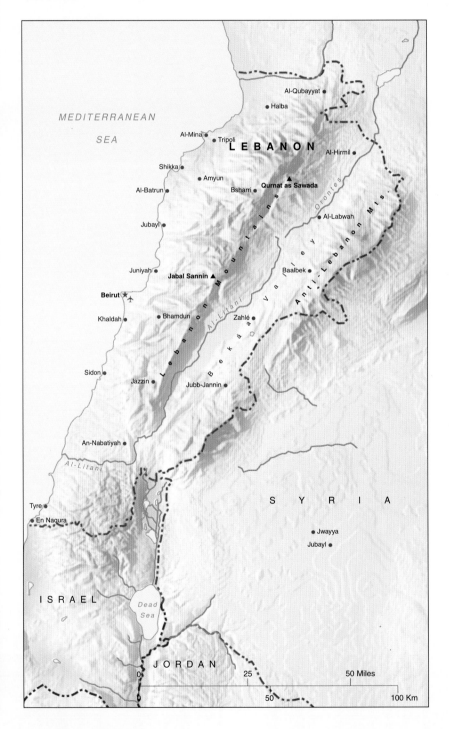

Above: Good soils, water from the hills, and an industrious workforce have made the narrow Bekáa Valley one of Lebanon's principal vegetable and fruit growing regions.

Right: The Lebanese capital of Beirut, on the eastern coast of the Mediterranean Sea, has a population of over 700,000. In the past, it was one of the leading cultural and commercial centers of the Middle East, and even after years of conflict it remains a significant trade and business center.

Israel and Jordan

Israel

Status:	Republic
Area:	8,130 square miles
Population:	6.1 million
Capital:	Jerusalem
Languages:	Hebrew, Arabic, English, Yiddish
Currency:	Shekel (100 agorot)

Four contrasting regions comprise Israel's landscape. A narrow fertile coastal plain fronts the Mediterranean Sea. Its northern section broadens around the Qishon River in the Plain of Esdraelon, where farmers grow grain, cotton, and vegetables. South of the Qishon, the drier Plain of Sharon supports the country's citrus farmers but must be irrigated.

The rolling hills of Galilee dominate north central Israel. Rich dark soils and plentiful rainfall sustain highly productive commercial gardens, where farmers grow vegetables and flowers for both local use and export.

The Jordan River Valley, running north to south from the Sea of Galilee to the Dead Sea, marks much of Israel's border with Jordan. Lying 1,300 feet below sea level, the Dead Sea is the lowest point on the earth's surface. It has no outlet and is the world's saltiest inland sea, providing Israel with a source of bromine, potash, and salt. The Jordan Valley is dry and not naturally fertile. Irrigating near the river and draining the marshy area north of the Sea of Galilee have created more fertile agricultural land.

The arid plateau of the Negev Desert covers southern Israel. Very little rain falls in this triangular-shaped region. Farmers in the desert's north raise fruits, vegetables, tomatoes, and **fodder crops** for dairy herds. Their fields are irrigated with water drawn from the Jordan River and from the streams that drain the southern coastal plain.

Almost 90 percent of Israelis live in urban areas, nearly a quarter of them in the three largest cities—Jerusalem, Tel Aviv-Jaffa, and Haifa. Factory workers in the industrial areas around Tel Aviv-Jaffa, Haifa, and the deepwater port of Ashdod produce chemicals, household goods, electronic equipment, scientific instruments,

paper, plastics, fertilizers, and textiles. Miners in the Negev Desert extract oil, copper, and phosphates, and a pipeline carries imported oil from Elat on the Gulf of Aqaba to a refinery at Haifa. Despite having to import most of its fuel and raw materials, Israel is the most industrialized country in the Middle East.

The State of Israel was created in 1948 from part of the former territory of Palestine. Neighboring Arab countries and displaced Palestinians opposed the new state, and Israel's short history has been one of constant wars. Signs of a negotiated peace only began to emerge in the late 1990s. Since 1967 Israel has occupied the West Bank (an area west of the Jordan River), the Gaza Strip (Egyptian territory), and the Golan Heights (Syrian territory). Israel removed its troops from a defensive buffer zone inside the southern border of Lebanon in 2000.

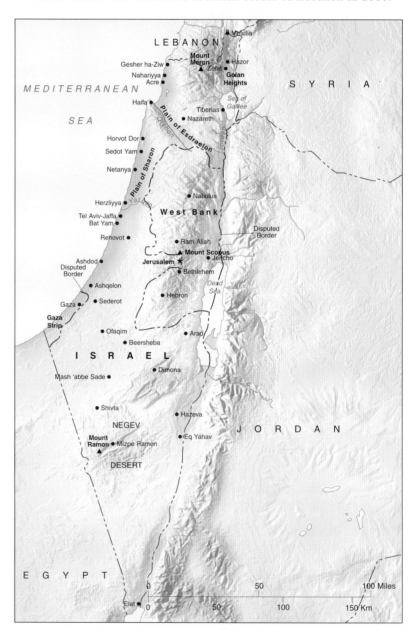

Jordan

Above: Jerusalem, Israel, is a holy city to Jews, Christians, and Muslims alike. The beautiful Dome of the Rock (foreground) is the city's holiest Muslim shrine.

Status:	Constitutional Monarchy
Area:	37,738 square miles
Population:	4.7 million
Capital:	Amman
Languages:	Arabic, English
Currency:	Jordanian dinar (1,000 fils)

The Hashemite Kingdom of Jordan does not have the oil wealth enjoyed by some neighboring Arab states. Its developing economy is based on the service industry, agriculture, and mining and is also supported by foreign aid.

The country has three principal land regions. In the west lies the Jordan River Valley. The land is not very fertile, but farmers are able to grow fruits and vegetables on fields irrigated by river water. To the south, the land rises to the Transjordan Plateau, a rolling upland region containing many of Jordan's largest cities and towns and most of its best farmland. Barley, wheat, citrus fruits, olives, and vegetables are the principal crops covering the northern plateau. The southern plateau region is very dry, supporting only small crops of wheat and olives. Northeastern Jordan lies on the Syrian Desert, which sees less than 10 inches of rain annually, and summer temperatures soar to 120°F. Few people live here apart from small groups of nomadic goat and sheep herders.

Many Jordanians work in neighboring countries. About 70 percent of those who remain in Jordan work for the government, for the military, or in various service industries such as education, banking, or the hotels and restaurants that support the growing numbers of tourists visiting the country's ancient sites.

Mines in the plateau region produce potash and phosphates, which are turned into fertilizers for export. Fertilizers, cement, and refining of imported oil comprise Jordan's only large-scale industries. Smaller factories in the plateau towns produce leather goods and textiles, processed food, pharmaceuticals, and some chemicals. Power for these industries comes from imported oil.

Above: The barren wilderness of the desert surrounds Mount Ramm (5,755 feet) in southwestern Jordan.

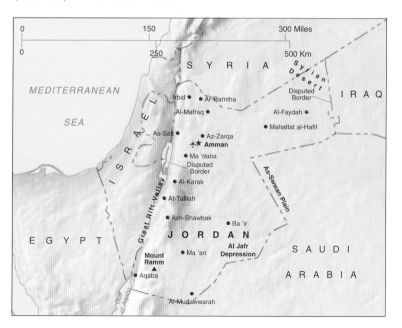

Iraq

Iraq

Status:	Republic
Area:	169,235 square miles
Population:	22.5 million
Capital:	Baghdad
Languages:	Arabic, Kurdish
Currency:	Iraqi dinar (1,000 fils)

Iraq is split in three by the Euphrates and Tigris Rivers—waterways that once supported the world's oldest known civilization. Farming communities occupied Sumer, in what would become southeastern Iraq, about 3500 B.C. The great city of Babylon—at the heart of the Babylonian Empire—flourished on the Euphrates's fertile banks from about 2200 B.C. until 539 B.C., when it was overthrown by Persian invaders.

The Zagros Mountains dominate northeastern Iraq, rising to more than 10,000 feet above sea level as they extend toward northern Iran and southeastern Turkey. Bitterly cold winters and just 15 inches of annual rainfall create a harsh environment for the local people.

Dry, rolling hills cover the northern plains between the Tigris and Euphrates Rivers. Farmers in the small, scattered villages grow wheat and barley on the productive soil that collects in the hollows and valleys. Sheep and goats graze on the surrounding dry grasslands. Southward from the capital city of Baghdad is an area between the two great rivers that provides Iraq's most fertile farmland. Farmers on the great southern plain grow grains, rice, fruit, and vegetables, irrigating their fields with water from the Tigris and Euphrates through a complex system of dams, channels, and control sluices. The two rivers meet at Al Qurnah, forming the Shatt al Arab. This channel flows southward to the Persian Gulf, where its delta forms Iraq's only stretch of coastline. Some of Iraq's most productive oil fields lie in this region, between the city of Basra and Iraq's border with Kuwait. Southeastern Iraq is a vast area of marshland and swamps.

Desert covers most of southwestern and western Iraq in a wilderness of sand dunes and bare limestone rock that stretches deep into Syria, Jordan, and Saudi Arabia. As in most deserts, there are no permanent rivers, just *wadis* (dry river channels) that briefly fill after a rainfall but dry out again almost immediately. The land is empty except for groups of Bedouin nomads and their camels, sheep, and goats.

Iraqis manufacture natural gas, phosphates, sulfur, cement, iron and steel, textiles, ceramics, chemicals, and household goods, but oil has been the country's economic mainstay for many years. Oil revenues helped improve schools, hospitals, roads, and the irrigation systems used to water the farms of Iraq's southern plains.

Much of that progress, however, was destroyed by war. A conflict with neighboring Iran, from 1980 until 1988, and the Gulf War, which followed Iraq's invasion of Kuwait in 1990, left Iraq's roads, bridges, oil refineries, factories, phone system, and parts of the main cities in ruins. Recovery has been hampered by international **trade sanctions** that were imposed when Iraq refused to cooperate with UN arms inspectors sent in under a cease-fire agreement.

Right: Traditional reed dwellings of the Marsh Arabs of southeastern Iraq

Opposite top: Kazimiya, Shrine of the Seventh and Ninth **Imams,** in Baghdad. With a population of almost six million, Baghdad is one of the largest cities in the Middle East. As far back as A.D. 800, it had over a million residents and was a world center of learning, culture, and religion. It contains some of the most beautiful mosques in the Islamic world.

Above: Muslim pilgrims sit in the quiet shade of the ornately decorated Pilgrimage Shrine in Karbala.

Opposite bottom: One of the many hundreds of oil pumping stations that dot the deserts of Iraq

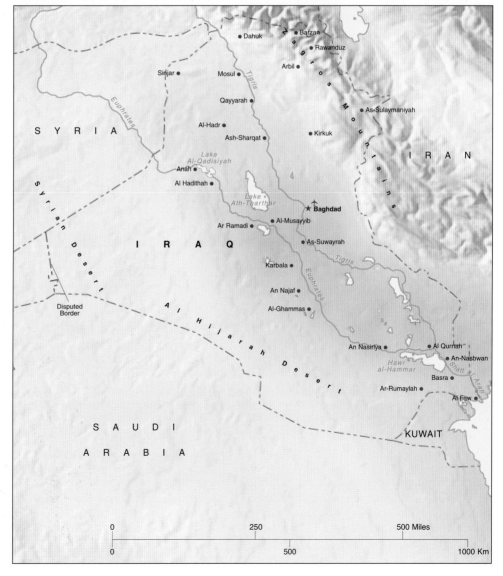

Iran

Iran

Status:	Republic
Area:	630,577 square miles
Population:	66.2 million
Capital:	Tehran
Languages:	Farsi (Persian), Arabic, Azeri-Turkish, Kurdish, Baluch
Currency:	Iranian rial (10 dinars)

Iran is an ancient land with a history dating back 5,000 years. Around 550 B.C., Iran (then known as Persia) was the center of an empire stretching across southwestern Asia, southern Europe, and part of North Africa. For much of the twentieth century, powerful shahs (kings) ruled the country. The last shah, Mohammad Reza Pahlavi, was forced into exile in 1979 by an Islamic revolution that brought to power the religious leader **Ayatollah** Ruhollah Khomeini. The ayatollah died in 1989, and more moderate politicians took charge of the government.

Fundamentalist clerics still have enormous influence in Iran's affairs. Women in particular have felt the effect. The rise of fundamentalism swept away all signs of modernization, such as free speech, relaxing of traditional dress codes, and relaxing of the strict rules governing women's lives. While Iran's large cities have schools, hospitals, and other amenities, most small rural communities have few of these benefits, and most houses do not have running water or electricity.

A desert plateau, 3,000 feet above sea level, dominates central and eastern Iran. North of the plateau, the rugged Elburz Mountains tower over a narrow coastal plain bordering the Caspian Sea. Mount Damavand, Iran's highest peak, rises to 18,984 feet in this range. West of the plateau, the broad Zagros range forms a mountainous barrier between Iran and Iraq. Lesser mountain ranges ring the eastern and southern margins of the plateau. Iran's central desert area is one of the driest, most barren places on earth. Few people live there. A narrow coastal plain on the shores of the Caspian Sea and a small fertile lowland area at the head of the Persian Gulf provide Iran's only good agricultural land. Farmers supplement

the principal crops of wheat and barley with lentils, cotton, sugar beets, fruits, vegetables, and tea. Farmers use less fertile land to raise cattle, sheep, and goats. Water is always in short supply in the south. The Caspian coastal plain is the only region that enjoys plentiful rain and a mild climate. Many of Iran's cities depend for their water on a labyrinth of tunnels and reservoirs that tap underground water supplies and catch what little rain falls inland.

Oil and gas are Iran's most important natural resources. The country is one of the world's top ten oil producers, and its gas reserves are second only to those of Russia. But Iran's war with Iraq from 1980 to 1988 and continuing internal political instability have greatly reduced its oil exports. The country supplements its economy by mining copper, chromite, iron ore, lead, and zinc. Factory workers manufacture machines, cement, chemicals, petroleum products, processed foods, textiles, and leather goods. Fishing fleets roam the Persian Gulf and the Caspian Sea in search of tuna, sardines, shrimp, carp, salmon, and sturgeon—a huge fish whose eggs yield the tiny, crunchy delicacy called **caviar.** Most of the fish is consumed locally, but the caviar is a valuable export.

Right: Two worlds meet in the Iranian desert—with oil wells of the industrial age towering over a livestock herder whose way of life goes back thousands of years.

Far right: Wool dyers in Esfahan prepare sheep and goat wool for the country's textile industries.

Left: Worshipers and visitors gather outside the magnificent Shrine of Fatimeh in Qom.

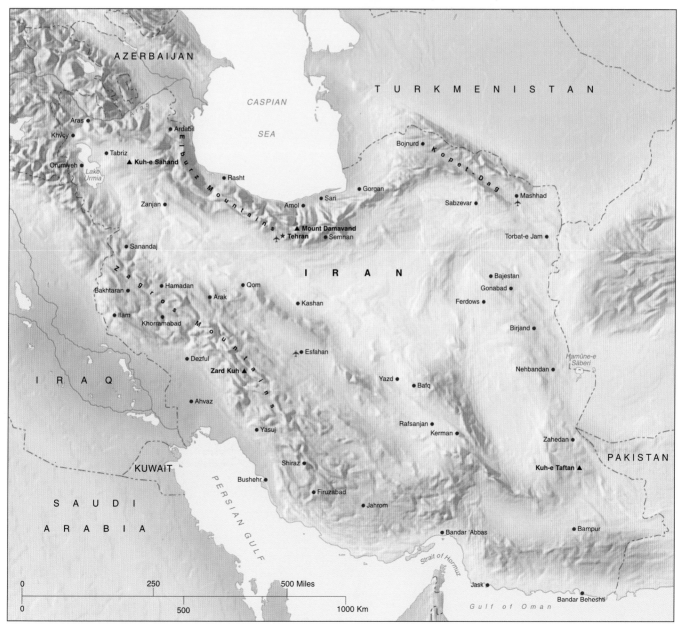

AZERBAIJAN

TURKMENISTAN

CASPIAN
SEA

Aras
Khvoy
• Ardabil
• Tabriz
▲ Kuh-e Sahand
Orumiyeh •
Lake
Urmia

Bojnurd •

K o p e t   D a g

• Rasht

Zanjan •

• Gorgan

Amol • • Sari

Sabzevar •
★ Mashhad

Sanandaj •

▲ Mount Damavand
✈ ★ Tehran   • Semnan

I R A N

Torbat-e Jam •

Z
a
g
r
o
s

M
o
u
n
t
a
i
n
s

Bakhtaran •

• Hamadan
• Arak   • Qom

Ilam •
Khorramabad •

• Kashan

• Bajestan
Gonabad •
Ferdows •

Birjand •

I R A Q

• Dezful
Zard Kuh ▲

✈ Esfahan

Yazd •
• Bafq

Nehbandan •

Hamûne-e
Sâberi

• Ahvaz

Rafsanjan •
Kerman •

Zahedan •

PAKISTAN

KUWAIT

• Yasuj

Shiraz •

P
E
R
S
I
A
N

G
U
L
F

Bushehr •

Firuzabad •

Kuh-e Taftan ▲

S A U D I
A R A B I A

• Jahrom

• Bandar 'Abbas

• Bampur

0   250   500 Miles

0   500   1000 Km

Strait of Hormuz

Jask •

Gulf of Oman

Bandar Beheshti •

Saudi Arabia and Kuwait

Saudi Arabia

Status:	Monarchy
Area:	829,996 square miles
Population:	20.9 million
Capital:	Riyadh
Languages:	Arabic, English
Currency:	Saudi riyal (100 halalas)

Saudi Arabia is the largest country in the Middle East, but more than 95 percent of its land is desert. A vast rocky plateau stretches across the country's middle. This area is dotted with **oases**—the most fertile of which support farming communities that grow dates, melons, vegetables, wheat, and other crops.

A broad area of sand dunes called An-Nafud lies north of the plateau, merging with the stony Syrian Desert on Saudi Arabia's borders with Jordan and Iraq. South of the plateau, bare rock and patchy vegetation meet a seemingly endless sea of sand dunes. Some of the mounds reach almost 1,000 feet in height. This is the Rub al-Khali (Empty Quarter)—the largest unbroken expanse of sand on earth. The only settlements are a few scattered oases. Most of the desert's inhabitants are nomadic Bedouin herders who travel constantly with their camels, goats, and sheep to find grazing land.

Mountains dominate western Saudi Arabia. They rise sharply from the northern Red Sea, dip slightly as they go south, and rise again to more than 10,000 feet near the border with Yemen. A narrow coastal plain lies between the mountains and the warm waters of the Red Sea. Asir—the southern part of the plain—is the most fertile region in Saudi Arabia.

Roughly three-quarters of the population live in urban areas, such as the capital city of Riyadh in east central Saudi Arabia and in Jidda, Al-Maqnah, and the Islamic holy cities of Mecca and Medina. More than 1.5 million pilgrims make the journey to Mecca every year. Nearly all Saudis are Muslims and are expected to make the *hajj,* or pilgrimage to Mecca, at least once in their life. The country's only non-Muslim residents are foreign-born people who work mostly in the oil fields and in communications, in construction, and in financial industries.

Saudi Arabia is the world's leading oil producer. Thirty years of multibillion-dollar oil revenues have allowed the government to fund a massive modernization program—building schools, colleges, hospitals, airports, and seaports and investing heavily in new industries and agricultural improvements.

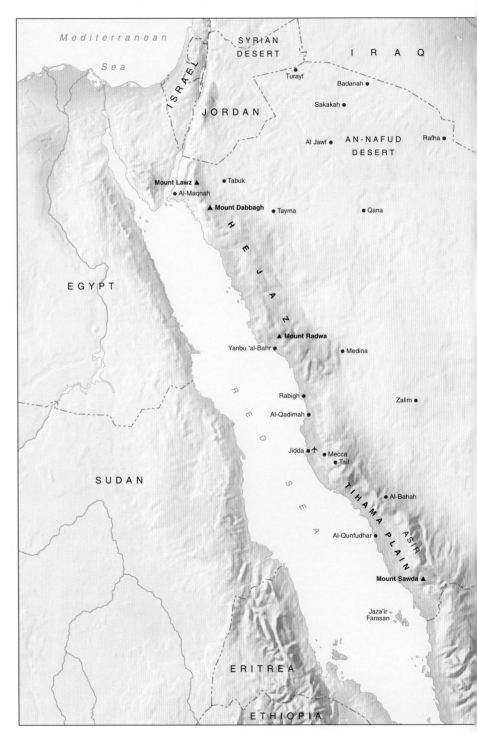

Kuwait

Status:	Constitutional Monarchy
Area:	6,880 square miles
Population:	2.1 million
Capital:	Kuwait City
Languages:	Arabic, English
Currency:	Kuwaiti dinar (100 fils)

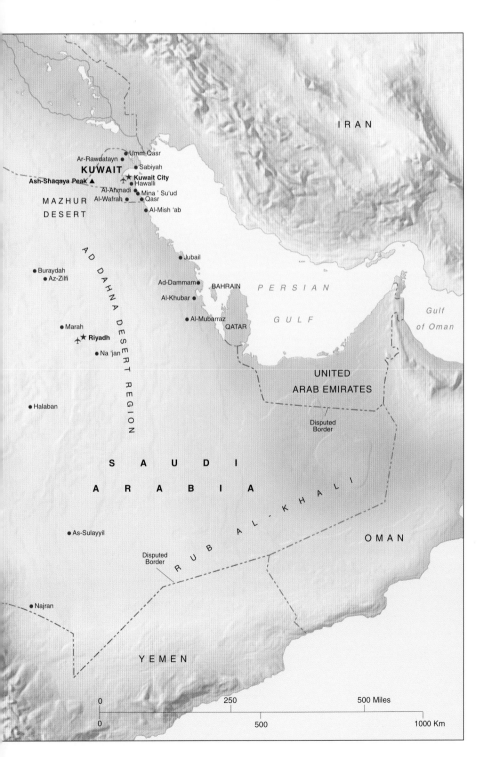

Tiny Kuwait is dwarfed by its enormous neighbors, Iraq and Saudi Arabia, but this small wedge of land on the northwestern shore of the Persian Gulf accounts for about one-tenth of the world's known oil reserves.

Kuwait's oil-related wealth has caused conflict. In response to an oil-pricing dispute, Iraq invaded Kuwait in 1990. Saudi Arabia, fearing an Iraqi invasion on its own territory, assisted Kuwait in forcing out Iraq. A UN-sponsored force eventually freed Kuwait. Although Iraq formally abandoned its claims to Kuwaiti territory in 1994, relations between the two countries have remained strained. Saudi Arabia and Kuwait, on the other hand, have grown closer.

Rainfall is sparse, and most of Kuwait consists of flat, stony desert, where temperatures rise to 104°F in summer. Farmers are able to take advantage of a small coastal strip with milder conditions and a little more rain, but much of the country's food must be imported.

Kuwaitis benefit from free education and health services and no taxes. Women enjoy more freedom and opportunity than they do in many neighboring Arab states. A serious lack of water was eased when the government used oil export revenues to install desalination plants, which turn seawater into fresh water. In 1960 further sources of fresh water were discovered deep underground.

Kuwait is a Muslim country, but laws forbid discrimination against non-Muslims. The country has an unusually varied population for an Islamic state. Arabs from several other Middle East countries live in Kuwait, alongside large numbers of Pakistanis and Indians, many of whom work on the country's numerous big construction projects.

Bahrain, Qatar, United Arab Emirates

Bahrain

Status:	Emirate
Area:	268 square miles
Population:	700,000
Capital:	Manama
Languages:	Arabic, English
Currency:	Bahraini dinar (1,000 fils)

Qatar

Status:	Emirate
Area:	4,247 square miles
Population:	500,000
Capital:	Doha
Languages:	Arabic, English
Currency:	Qatari riyal (100 dirhams)

Bahrain is a cluster of more than 30 islands in the Persian Gulf, about 20 miles off the eastern tip of Saudi Arabia. The country's capital city, Manama, sits at the northern end of Bahrain Island—the largest and most populated island of the group. A paved causeway provides a direct link to the Saudi Arabian mainland.

Desert covers most of the islands. Before the discovery of petroleum in 1932, Bahrain was poor and underdeveloped. Oil revenues have turned the country into one of the richest in the world. Bahrainis have a very high standard of living. Most people live in comfortable apartments with air conditioning and refrigerators. Education is free, and the country has hundreds of schools, including two universities. Health services are excellent, and the people enjoy a healthy diet of fish, rice, vegetables, and fruit—especially dates.

Rainfall is sparse, averaging just three inches annually, but numerous freshwater springs and wells provide plenty of water for domestic use and for irrigation of the fertile farmland found on northern Bahrain Island. Oil refining is the main industrial activity. The huge refinery on Sitrah Island keeps busy processing the country's petroleum as well as oil delivered by pipeline from Saudi Arabia. Other industries include ship repair, chemicals, and aluminum products, and Bahrain is the major banking center for the Persian Gulf region.

The tiny Arab nation of Qatar occupies a rocky desert peninsula that juts into the Persian Gulf. Saudi Arabia and the United Arab Emirates are Qatar's mainland neighbors. Discovery of oil in the 1940s transformed Qatar from a poor nation of camel herders, **subsistence farmers,** and pearl divers into a wealthy urbanized nation with free education and health services and a very high standard of living.

Oil revenues paid for desalination plants to provide fresh water for homes, hotels, offices, and industrial areas and enabled the government to sink many deep wells to provide water for irrigation. Qatari farmers meet most of the country's vegetable needs and provide some of its grain and fruit, but meat, dairy products, and many manufactured goods are imported. The government owns most of Qatar's industries, which range from oil refining and petrochemicals to commercial fishing, fertilizer production, and plastics.

Above left: Oil tankers are being loaded at a deepwater jetty in Qatar.

Above: One of the many large oil storage facilities in the United Arab Emirates

Right: A traditional bazaar (market) in Abu Dhabi

United Arab Emirates

Status:	Federation of Seven Emirates
Area:	32,278 square miles
Population:	2.8 million
Capital:	Abu Dhabi
Languages:	Arabic, English
Currency:	UAE dirham (100 fils)

The United Arab **Emirates** is a **federation** of seven independent states bordering the southern shore of the Persian Gulf. The member-states and their capital cities, from west to east, are Abu Dhabi, Dubayy, Ash Shariqah, Ajman, Umm al Qaywayn, Ras al Khaymah, and Al Fujayrah. Abu Dhabi is the federation's capital and second largest city. Dubayy is the largest urban area and the federation's principal port and business center. Formerly a British **protectorate,** the seven countries were once called the Trucial States. Six of the states gained independence in 1971 and were joined by the seventh, Ras al Khaymah, the following year.

The countries that formed the United Arab Emirates, like its neighbor Qatar, used to be dependent on camel herding, fishing, trading, and subsistence farming. Life for its people changed dramatically with the discovery of oil in the 1950s. The modern federation has one of the world's highest standards of living.

Yemen and Oman

Yemen

Status:	Republic
Area:	203,850 square miles
Population:	16.4 million
Capital:	Sana'a
Language:	Arabic
Currency:	Yemeni rial (100 fils)

Shaped like a fat check mark cradling the southern edge of Saudi Arabia, Yemen occupies the southwestern corner of the Arabian Peninsula. Yemen's territory includes the Red Sea islands of Kamaran and Perim and Socotra Island in the Arabian Sea. Modern Yemen was formed in 1990 by the joining of two separate nations—South Yemen and North Yemen. South Yemen tried to pull out in 1994, and bitter fighting erupted. Peace was restored, with UN help, but relations between the south and the dominant north remain strained.

Yemen consists of rugged mountains in the west and a desert in the east that spreads northward into Saudi Arabia's Rub al-Khali. Temperatures are very hot and humid along the narrow coastal plain, but the country enjoys cooler, milder conditions in the highlands, where fertile valleys provide Yemen's best farmland. Yemenis cultivate crops in the highlands and on scattered desert oases, and they graze sheep, goats, and camels in the drier desert areas. Fishing crews ply the abundant waters along the coastline.

A large oil refinery at Aden processes oil from Yemeni fields in the northwest, as well as oil from other Persian Gulf states. The government has used oil revenues to boost agriculture—building dams and irrigation projects—and to provide the population with improved schools, medical facilities, and housing. Aden is home to one of the region's main trading ports, providing repair yards and other services for ship operators. Construction projects are the other main employer, but hundreds of small factories and local craftspeople produce handmade brass and copper goods, saddles and harnesses, pottery, jewelry, and the ornate daggers (*jambiyas*) that form part of traditional Arab dress.

Left: The minaret of a mosque overlooks the town of Raydah in the western part of Yemen.

Oman

Status:	Monarchy
Area:	82,000 square miles
Population:	2.5 million
Capital:	Masqat
Languages:	Arabic, local dialects
Currency:	Omani rial (100 baizas)

Oman curves around the southeastern corner of the Arabian Peninsula, exposing a long coastline on the Arabian Sea and a short stretch of coastline facing Iran across the Gulf of Oman. The narrow **Strait of Hormuz,** off Oman's northernmost tip, guards the entrance to the Persian Gulf. Much of the world's oil is shipped through this narrow seaway.

Oman shares its borders with Yemen, Saudi Arabia, and the United Arab Emirates. Similar to its neighbors, Oman is mostly desert. One of the earth's hottest areas, the country often sees temperatures rise to 120°F, sometimes soaring above 130°F. Rainfall is meager. Most villages draw their water from deep wells, some of them part of a canal system from ancient times. The land is very dry, and farmers in small, scattered villages struggle to grow enough grain, vegetables, and fruit to meet their needs. Camels, goats, and sheep provide meat, milk, and hides for leather. Along the coast, most Omanis work in fisheries or on large date palm plantations. Alfalfa, coconuts, onions, tomatoes, and wheat prosper in the most fertile areas.

Oman embraces its history and cultural ways. Most of the people wear traditional dress and nearly all are devout Muslims. Money from oil exports funds an ongoing program to build schools and adult education centers, but literacy levels lag behind those of many Persian Gulf states.

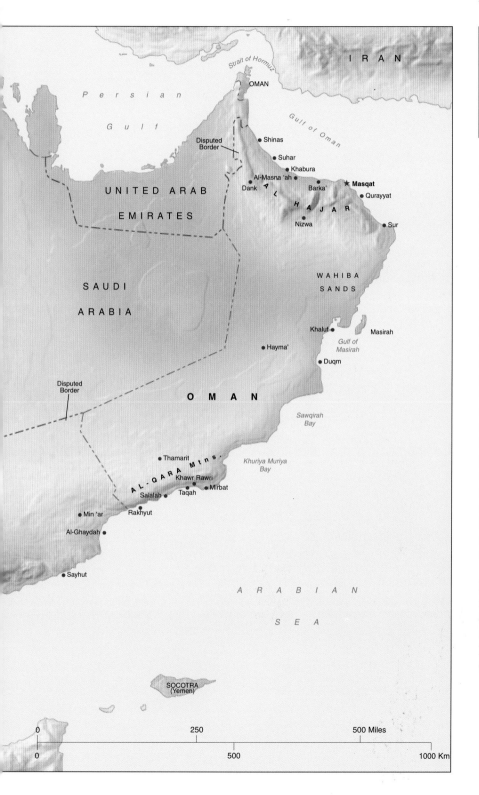

Russian Federation (Asian Russia)

Russian Federation

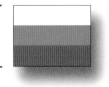

Status:	Federation
Area:	6,592,819 square miles
Population:	146.5 million
Capital:	Moscow
Language:	Russian
Currency:	Russian ruble (100 kopeks)

Russia is the largest country in the world. Even after losing 14 of the 15 republics that comprised the former Soviet Union, Russia is still nearly twice the size of the United States. The Russian Federation stretches 6,000 miles from the borders of Norway, Finland, and the Baltic States in the west to the Pacific Ocean in the east. It extends almost 2,800 miles from the Arctic Ocean to the borders of Kazakhstan, Mongolia, and China.

Russia traces its history to the medieval Slavic state of Kievan Rus, which covered most of modern Ukraine, Belarus, and European Russia. Mongol invaders from central Asia destroyed Kievan Rus in the thirteenth century. In the 1300s, a new state called Muscovy took its place and was succeeded in the 1700s by the Russian Empire. The Russian Revolution of 1917 ended imperial rule, replacing it with a Communist government, which remained in power until 1991.

During the 1990s, Russians suffered great hardships. The country tried to change from the Communist system—under which the government controlled everything—to a free-market economy where people can own their own companies and compete with one another for business.

Right: Vladivostok, on the southeastern coast of Siberia, is Russia's most important Pacific seaport. Shipyards, fish canneries, and factories producing mining equipment and other heavy machinery are the principal employers.

The Russian Federation
East and West of the Urals

Above: Asian Russia—east of the Urals—is almost three times the size of the country's European segment. Russia is a sparsely populated land of plains, plateaus, and forests. A train journey from Moscow to Vladivostok takes seven days and passes through eight time zones.

ARCTIC OCEAN

Franz
Josef Land

Wrangel I.

Saint Lawrence I.
(U.S.)

Bering Strait

Mys Shmidta

Chukchi Peninsula

East
Siberian
Sea

Pevek
Ayon I.

Gulf of
Anadyr

Anadyr

Bering
Sea

Komsomolets I.

New Siberia I.

Bilibino

Koryak Mountains

October
Revolution I.

Bol'shevik I.

Kotel'nyy I.
New Siberian Is.
Lyakhovskiye
Ostrova

Nizhnekolymsk

Kolyma Mountains

Kara
Sea

Laptev
Sea

Bol'shoy
Begichev I.

Novosibirsk

Srednekolymsk

Korf

Novaya Zemlya

Belyy I.

Byrranga Mtns.

Tiksi

Kolyma

Indigirka

Karagin I.

Palana

Kamchatka Peninsula

North Siberian
Lowland

Cherskiy Range

East

Lena

Verkhoyanskiy Khrebet

Oimyakon

Magadan

Petropavlovsk-
Kamchatskiy

Noril'sk

Central

Udachnyy

Siberian

Okhotsk

Sea of
Okhotsk

Igarka

Siberian

Sangar

Nadym

Yakutsk

Nyurba

Highlands

Gulf of Ob

Yenisey

Lower Tunguska

Mirnyy

Lena

Tura

Dzhugdzhur Range

West

Plateau

Lensk

Aldan

Surgut

RUSSIA

Kuril Islands

Siberian

Sakhalin I.

Nizhnevartovsk

Angara

Neryungri

Badzhal'skiy Mtns.

Komsomol'sk
na-Amure

Sakhalin I.

Plain

Bodaybo

Tynda

Amur

Sikhote-alin Mtns.

Tatar Strait

Ob

Krasnoyarsk

Ust'-Ilimsk

Zeya

Yuzhno-
Sakhalinsk

Tomsk

Ust'-Kut

Shimanovsk

Soya Strait

Omsk

Kemerovo

Bratsk

Bratsk
Reservoir

Khabarovsk

Novosibirsk

Lake
Baikal

Yablonovyy Range

Amur

Blagoveshchensk

Vyazemskiy

Nerchinsk

Barnaul

Novokuznetsk

Ust-Ordinskiy

Chita

Baley

Abakan

Angarsk

Irkutsk

Ulan Ude

Spassk-Dal 'niy

Prokopyevsk

Sayan Mtns.

Munku-Sardyk

Aginskoyo

Borzya

Ussurlysk

Kyzyl

Yenisey

Kyakhta

Vladivostok

Nakhodka

KAZAKHSTAN

J
A
P
A
N

MONGOLIA

Sea of
Japan

NORTH
KOREA

SOUTH
KOREA

CHINA

0   500   1000   1500 Miles

0   500   1000   1500   2000   2500 Km

Russian Federation (Asian Russia)

Climate and vegetation define four broad zones that stretch west to east across Asian Russia. The extreme northern reaches support a bleak landscape of mosses, shrubs, and dwarf trees called tundra. The soil is permanently frozen, and winters are long and harsh. Summers offer a brief respite, during which the soil's surface thaws and some vegetation grows—enough to feed reindeer, hares, lemmings, and ptarmigan and the wolves, foxes, stoats, owls, and hawks that hunt them.

Dark **coniferous** forests of pine, fir, and spruce lie south of the tundra, merging into **deciduous** forests of birch, oak, aspen, and maple. Deer, elk, beavers, brown bears, and squirrels are typical forest animals. Rolling grassy plains called the steppes stretch across Russia south of the forests. Thick dark soils in this region provide Russia's best farmland. The steppes offer little cover from predators. Animals able to survive here are those that burrow—hamsters, susliks, lemmings, and marmots—and the eagles and

Left: Oil pipelines run for hundreds of miles across the forested landscape, carrying crude oil from the Siberian oil fields to European Russia, where demand for energy is greatest and where the largest refineries are located. The zigzag construction allows the pipeline to expand and contract without cracking as temperatures rise and fall.

buzzards that patrol the skies. Deserts and mountains dominate Russia's southern edge, forming natural borders with its huge southern neighbors—Kazakhstan, Mongolia, and China.

Asian Russia has three major land divisions—the West Siberian Plain, the Central Siberian Plateau, and the East Siberian Highlands. The Urals form a long, narrow north-south barrier between European Russia and the westernmost Asian Russian landform—the West Siberian Plain. East of the mountains, the West Siberian Plain stretches for nearly 1,000 miles. The northern section of the plain is low and marshy. In the southern section, farmers use the fertile soil to raise barley, oats, rye, potatoes, sugar beets, fruits and vegetables, and fodder crops for beef and dairy cattle. The plain also contains rich oil and gas fields, and miners take out coal, iron ore, lead, and zinc from deposits along the mountainous southern edge. Omsk, Novosibirsk, Tomsk, and Novokuznetsk are the main manufacturing centers of the West Siberian Plain.

The Central Siberian Plateau lies east of the Yenisey River. The topography ranges from 2,000 feet above sea level to 11,451 at the top of Munku-Sardyk, the tallest peak in the Sayan Mountains. Forests cover much of the land. The plateau lies in the heart of the huge Asian landmass, far from any moderating effects of the ocean. In winter it is one of the coldest places on earth. January temperatures in northeastern Siberia average below -50°F and can plunge to -90°F. Few people live in this region's far north, but industrial cities such as Krasnoyarsk and Irkutsk have developed in the south, where miners extract gold, nickel, tungsten, tin, and other minerals.

Beyond the Lena River, the land rises to the East Siberian Highlands—a vast empty wilderness of pine forests and mountain ranges. The highlands stretch unbroken to the Chukchi Peninsula, which faces the United States across the narrow Bering Strait, and to the leaf-shaped and volcanic Kamchatka Peninsula that partly encloses the Sea of Okhotsk. Inhabitants of this region cluster around the inland city of Yakutsk, around Khabarovsk on the Amur River, and around the industrial city and seaport of Vladivostok on the Sea of Japan's northwestern coast.

Below: A huge roll of heavy packaging paper is hoisted off the production machine at a paper mill in Siberia.

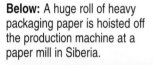

Kazakhstan

Kazakhstan

Status:	Republic
Area:	1.05 million square miles
Population:	15.4 million
Capital:	Astana
Languages:	Kazakh, Russian
Currency:	Tenge (100 tiyn)

One of western Asia's largest countries, Kazakhstan ranks ninth in the world in land area. In 1991 Kazakhstan gained its freedom from the Soviet Union after 70 years under Communist rule. Since becoming an independent **republic,** Kazakhstan's government has built a new capital, Astana, near the center of the country. Almaty, the former capital, lies close to the border with China and remains Kazakhstan's largest city and principal commercial and cultural center.

Kazakhstan extends almost 1,800 miles east to west, up to 900 miles north to south, and boasts a variety of landscapes. Dry lowland plains wrap around the northern tip of the Caspian Sea. The Karagiye Basin, between the coastal town of Aqtau and the Turkmenistan border, is the lowest point in the country at 433 feet below sea level. Rolling steppes cover much of northern Kazakhstan, and sandy deserts dominate the country's southern region. The rugged Altai Shan (mountains) rise on the country's northeastern border with Russia, and the Tian Shan form the southeastern border with Kyrgyzstan and China. Rivers rising in the mountains feed Lake Balkhash, the largest lake in the country at 6,670 square miles.

The dry grassy plains that cover much of the country are not well suited to farming. Most Kazakhs were traditionally nomads, traveling with the sheep, goats, camels, cattle, and horses that provided their transportation, food, and materials for clothing and shelter. The traditional Kazakh home was a portable tentlike structure, called a yurt, made of thick felt mats covering a frame of bent poles. The yurt provided a warm, windproof shelter in the bitterly cold winter and cool shade in the hot summer months. Some Kazakhs still live as their ancestors did, but most rural villagers live in houses.

Prime farmland lies in northeastern Kazakhstan where farmers sow barley, wheat, cotton, and vegetables and graze sheep, and beef and dairy herds. During the Communist era, Kazakhstan's government greatly expanded agricultural production by irrigating dry western lands with water from feeder rivers to the Aral Sea. While this enabled some farmers to grow rice, grain crops, and vegetables, the Aral Sea shrank by 70 percent. These irrigation projects left much of the former sea glistening with salt pans and littered with the rotting hulks of stranded fishing boats.

Kazakhstan is rich in mineral resources. Miners in the northeast extract coal, while those in the central and eastern regions mine copper, zinc, iron, lead, tin, titanium, vanadium, thallium, and other valuable minerals. Oil and gas are pumped from fields beneath the Caspian Sea.

Factories in the principal industrial towns of Almaty and Shymkent in the southeast and Karaganda and Pavlodar in the northeast provide textiles, chemicals, leather goods, machinery, electrical goods, and food products.

Right: A Kazakh horseman looks across the rolling forests and grasslands that supported his nomadic ancestors and their livestock for thousands of years.

Below left: Kazakhstan has a long tradition of creating fine buildings from its principal natural construction material—wood. This magnificent example stands in Almaty, the historic former capital and principal cultural center.

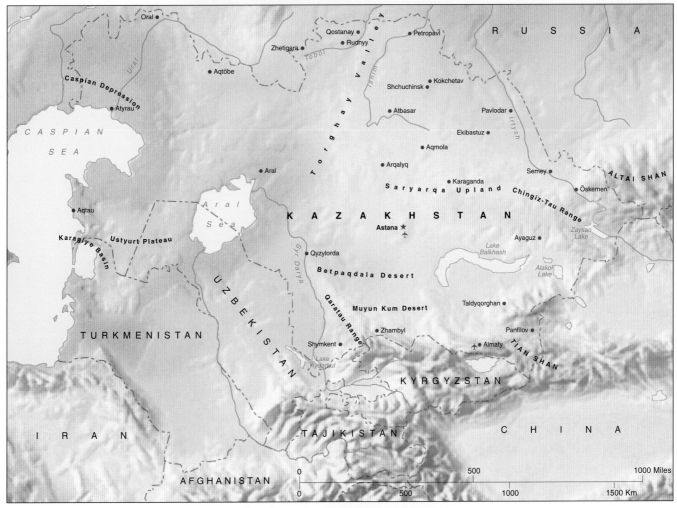

Uzbekistan and Turkmenistan

Uzbekistan

Status:	Republic
Area:	172,742 square miles
Population:	24.4 million
Capital:	Tashkent
Languages:	Uzbek, Russian
Currency:	Uzbek som (100 tijuns)

Uzbekistan lies in western central Asia and shares borders with Kazakhstan, Kyrgyzstan, Tajikistan, Turkmenistan, and Afghanistan. The latter is the only one of Uzbekistan's neighbors that wasn't a former Soviet republic.

The vast barren wilderness of the Kyzyl Kum Desert fills the country's center. Few people, apart from workers in scattered mining settlements, live in this region. Farther west, dry grasslands and deserts border the Aral Sea, merging with the arid plains and plateaus of Kazakhstan and Turkmenistan. Most inhabitants of western Uzbekistan live in small towns and villages clustered along the banks of the Amu Darya (River) and its tributaries.

About 80 percent of the Uzbeks are farmers, a fact that concentrates the population in southern and eastern Uzbekistan. The land in these areas rises to meet the Tian Shan and the Pamir Mountains. The region's rich soil and mountain streams support fertile crops such as rice, grains, vegetables, melons, and cotton—the country's principal export crop. Sheep and dairy cattle are significant livestock, supplying mutton and milk for the country's traditional dishes. The high-quality wool of the Karakul sheep is another important export.

Uzbekistan's miners extract coal, copper, gold, petroleum, and natural gas. Industrial contributions include textiles, chemicals, farm machinery, and fertilizers. Traditional craft workers in rural areas create carpets, shawls, jewelry, ceramics, wood products, and metal goods.

Turkmenistan

Status:	Republic
Area:	188,456 square miles
Population:	4.8 million
Capital:	Ashkhabad
Languages:	Turkmen, Russian, Uzbek
Currency:	Turkmenistan manat (100 tenge)

Dominated by the large, central Kara-Kum Desert, Turkmenistan is ringed by Kazakhstan, Uzbekistan, Afghanistan, Iran, and the Caspian Sea. The country's landscapes include low coastal plains hugging the Caspian Sea, mountains along the border with Iran, and the broad Amu Darya Valley forming the northern boundary with Uzbekistan. The Kara-Bogaz Gol, a deep gulf near the Caspian shore, is the country's lowest point at 102 feet below sea level. Summers are very hot, with temperatures reaching 120°F. Winters are bitterly cold. Thermometers hover near zero for many weeks. Rainfall is scarce, providing just a few inches annually to most of the country.

Small settlements are located at desert oases, but most Turkmen live by water—near the coast of the Caspian Sea, beside the 750-mile long Kara-Kum Canal, or in the irrigated highland river valleys. Farmers in these regions grow grains, vegetables, and grapes for local consumption, but more than half the cultivated land in Turkmenistan is committed to cotton, the country's principal crop. Many farmers supplement their crops by raising sheep, camels, pigs, and horses.

Turkmenistan's chief natural resources are oil and gas. The mining industry provides copper, lead, mercury, gold, and other minerals, including limestone and sand for Turkmen homes. Factories—concentrated around the capital city of Ashkhabad and in the city of Chardzhou—produce textiles, glassware, petrochemical products, and cement.

Right: A Turkmen woman wears a traditional costume of brightly patterned fabrics, a headdress, and handmade jewelry.

Far right: An Uzbek miner tends a large coal-cutting machine in one of the country's modern mines.

Below: An Uzbek elder wears the traditional wound cloth headdress known as a *termez*.

Kyrgyzstan and Tajikistan

Kyrgyzstan

Status:	Republic
Area:	76,641 square miles
Population:	4.7 million
Capital:	Bishkek
Languages:	Kyrgyz, Russian
Currency:	Kyrgyz som (100 tyin)

Tajikistan

Status:	Republic
Area:	55,251 square miles
Population:	6.2 million
Capital:	Dushanbe
Languages:	Tajik, Uzbek, Russian
Currency:	Tajik ruble (100 tanga)

Kyrgyzstan is a small, landlocked country high in the Tian Shan and the Alai Mountains of western central Asia. Rugged and inhospitable, three-quarters of the country sit more than 5,000 feet above sea level—most of it covered in glaciers and snowfields. Pobedy Peak, Kyrgyzstan's highest summit, towers 24,406 feet over the eastern border with China. Winter temperatures often fall to -20°F in the mountains. Sheltered valleys and lowlands experience warm, dry summers and cold winters. Rainfall is minimal, so the country taps mountain rivers for water to use on crops, in homes, and by the industrial sector.

The people of Kyrgyzstan once wandered across the lowlands and foothills, grazing their sheep, goats, pigs, cattle, and horses. Few people still follow the traditional nomadic ways, but livestock continues to be vital to the economy. Farmers grow cotton, rice, fruits, sugar beets and other vegetables, and mulberry—a tree whose leaves feed silkworms.

Kyrgyz miners extract the country's reserves of coal and minerals such as uranium, mercury, lead, gold, and zinc. The country also holds untapped oil reserves. Manufacturing industries, concentrated mostly around the capital city of Bishkek, use these resources to produce textiles, machinery, domestic appliances, and electronics. The government is expanding the industrial sector and attracting foreign investors, making Kyrgyzstan one of the fastest-growing economies among former Soviet republics.

Tajikistan, like its neighbor Kyrgyzstan to the north, is a rugged, mountainous country. Half of its land reaches 10,000 feet above sea level. The Pamir Mountains to the southeast form a border with Pakistan. The Zeravshan, Turkestan, and Alai Mountains dominate central and northern Tajikistan. The country's valleys and lowlands experience long, hot, dry summers and cool winters. Both urban and rural populations rely for water on the country's rivers. Irrigation projects in eastern and northern Tajikistan support the country's agriculture.

Cotton is Tajikistan's most significant commercial crop, but farmers also grow many fruits, vegetables, and grains. Cattle, chickens, and sheep provide meat, milk, eggs, wool, and leather, and domesticated yaks graze on the high mountain slopes. Some farms specialize in growing mulberry trees for silkworm farms, while others harvest eucalyptus, geraniums, and other plants whose oils and fragrances are used to make perfumes.

A huge dam at Nurek on the Vakhsh River supplies hydroelectric power to a large aluminum refinery and to other industries concentrated around the capital city of Dushanbe. The Nurek Reservoir provides water for the cities and farms of western Tajikistan. Tajik miners extract antimony, lead, tungsten, uranium, and zinc, and the country possesses large gold and silver reserves. Unlike neighboring Kyrgyzstan, economic development in Tajikistan has suffered throughout the 1990s from internal conflict and civil war.

Right: A few Kyrgyz families still follow the traditional ways, living in tentlike yurts and constantly moving from pasture to pasture with their livestock. The yurt, made of felt, is warm, comfortable, and immensely practical in the rugged conditions.

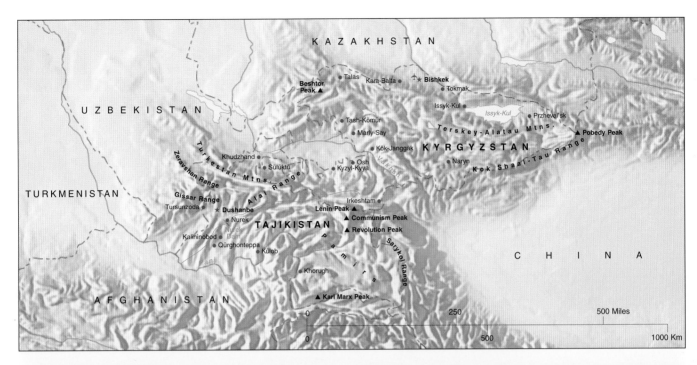

Georgia, Armenia, Azerbaijan

Georgia

Status:	Republic
Area:	26,911 square miles
Population:	5.4 million
Capital:	Tbilisi
Languages:	Georgian, Russian, Armenian
Currency:	Lari (100 tetri)

Armenia

Status:	Republic
Area:	11,506 square miles
Population:	3.8 million
Capital:	Yerevan
Languages:	Armenian, Russian
Currency:	Dram (100 luma)

Georgia broke away from the former Soviet Union in 1991. The country's independence has been marred by ethnic conflicts between the dominant Georgians, who comprise 70 percent of the population, and the peoples of South Ossetia, Abkhazia, and Adjaria who demand self-government for their regions. Years of unrest have damaged the country's economy and have slowed development.

Mountains dominate northern and southern Georgia. The broad, fertile Kura River Valley in central Georgia and the western lowland plains bordering the Black Sea provide excellent farmland. These areas have hot summers and mild winters and receive ample rainfall.

Farmers in the western plains grow citrus fruits, tea, and **tung trees,** whose seeds yield valuable oil used in paints and varnishes. Wheat, barley, and vegetables are the main crops farther inland. Many farmers also cultivate flowers and herbs for the perfume industry. Mulberry trees support a thriving silk industry. The soil on sunny hillsides produces grapes for making wine. Large forests in the mountainous regions provide raw materials for lumber and plywood factories.

Georgia's miners excavate many minerals, but food processing remains the country's primary industry, and food products are its main export. Coastal resorts along the Black Sea attract large numbers of tourists, many of them from neighboring Russia.

Right: Turkish-style bathhouses nestle among modern apartment blocks in the old sector of the Georgian capital of Tbilisi.

Nestled between Georgia, Azerbaijan, Iran, and Turkey, this tiny state is the smallest of the 15 former Soviet republics and one of five that declared independence in 1991. A mountainous plateau, 5,000 feet above sea level, covers most of the country. The plateau is dissected by deep river gorges and is dotted with towering peaks reaching higher than 12,000 feet above sea level. Armenia also boasts more than 100 lakes. Forests of beech, oak, and **hornbeam** blanket parts of Armenia's eastern mountains. Short grasses and scrub cover much of the rest.

Low rainfall in the valleys combined with short hot summers, very cold winters, and a lack of investment have kept agricultural productivity quite low. Farmers grow wheat, barley, potatoes, walnuts, and quinces and other fruits on fertile black soil in the valleys, but farming is most productive on irrigated land in the Araks River Valley on Armenia's borders with Turkey and Iran.

Vanadzor, Gyumri, and Yerevan in the northwest and Kapan in the southeast are important manufacturing centers. Hydroelectric power stations on fast-flowing rivers such as the Hrazdan provide power for the country's main industries—machinery, chemicals, electronics, and textiles. These industries, along with the copper, lead, and zinc produced by Armenia's miners, account for about two-thirds of Armenia's economic production.

Above: Roadside vendors sell fruit at Garni in Armenia.

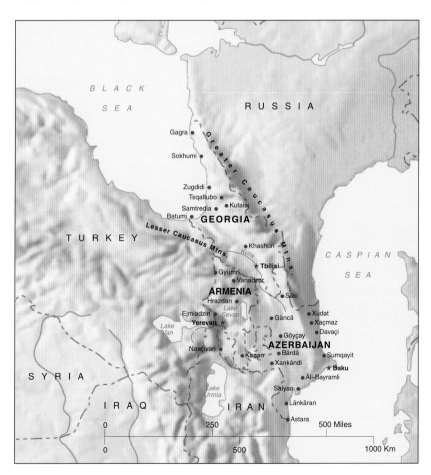

Status:	Republic
Area:	33,436 square miles
Population:	7.7 million
Capital:	Baku
Language:	Azeri Turkish
Currency:	Azeri manat (100 qepik)

Azerbaijan is divided into three distinct land regions. The Greater Caucasus Mountains run east to west near the country's northern edge, separating Azerbaijan from Georgia and Russia and marking a line between the continents of Europe and Asia. Rocky highlands rise in the west and southwest. Between the two highland regions, a broad, lowland plain slopes down to the Caspian Sea. The small autonomous republic of Naxçivan, which is geographically separate but still belongs politically to Azerbaijan, lies beyond Azerbaijan's southwestern border and is surrounded by Armenia.

Oil fields near the capital city of Baku and beneath the Caspian Sea provide Azerbaijan's principal source of income. The country also extracts aluminum, copper, iron, and salt. Factories in the main industrial centers of Baku, Gäncä, Säki, Xankändi, and Naxçivan produce aluminum, machinery, chemicals, textiles, cement, and timber products.

Azerbaijan depends heavily on its waterways. Hydroelectric stations use river water flowing from the surrounding mountains to power much of the country's industrial sector. Rivers also irrigate farms on the dry central plain, where rainfall is generally minimal. Lowland farmers grow grains, cotton, vegetables, fruits, and tea. Those in the upland regions raise sheep, goats, and cattle and grow fodder crops for winter animal feed.

Glossary

Arabian Peninsula: a vast, mostly desert area of southwestern Asia whose political divisions are Bahrain, Kuwait, Oman, Qatar, Saudi Arabia, the United Arab Emirates, and Yemen

ayatollah: a highly respected religious leader among Shiite Muslims

Bedouin: a member of the nomadic peoples who inhabit the desert areas of North Africa and the Middle East

caviar: an expensive food made from the salted eggs of certain large fish, such as sturgeon

coniferous: describing mainly evergreen trees that bear cones and have needle-shaped leaves

deciduous: describing trees that lose their leaves at some season of the year

emirate: a state under the rule of an emir, meaning "commander" or "chief" in Arabic

federation: a form of government in which states or groups unite under a central power. The states or groups surrender power to make some decisions but retain limited territorial control.

fodder crops: coarse plants—such as cornstalks, hay, and straw—that are grown as food for cattle, horses, and other farm animals

fundamentalist: adhering to a strict and literal interpretation of a set of beliefs

glacier: a large body of ice and snow that moves slowly over land

hajj: the journey to the Saudi Arabian city of Mecca, defined as one of the five religious duties each Muslim must try to perform

hornbeam tree: a member of the birch family, having gray bark and hard white wood

Imam: an Islamic leader who traces his descent from the prophet Muhammad. An Imam often holds civil as well as religious authority.

Middle East: an unofficial term to describe the countries of southwestern Asia and northeastern Africa

oasis: a fertile area of a desert that is usually fed by an underground source of water. Oases can vary in size from a small patch surrounded by date palms to a large city that raises yearly crops.

plateau: a large, relatively flat area that stands above the surrounding land

prevailing wind: the dominant wind, indicated by direction, in a certain place

protectorate: a territory under the authority of another

Ramadan: the ninth month of the Islamic year, observed by fasting from dawn to sunset every day

republic: a government having a chief of state (usually a president) who is not a monarch. In a republic, supreme power belongs to a body of citizens who are entitled to vote and who elect representatives responsible to the citizens. These representatives govern according to law.

Semite: a member of any of the historic or modern peoples of southwestern Asia who speaks a Semitic language, such as Hebrew or Arabic

steppes: the level, generally treeless grasslands of Russia, eastern Europe, and central Asia

Strait of Hormuz: the strategically important transportation route that connects the Persian Gulf with the Gulf of Oman and the Indian Ocean. After having their holds filled with oil, tankers navigate the strait to bring the fuel to destinations throughout the world.

subsistence farmer: one who grows only enough crops to feed the family, with little, if any, surplus for market

trade sanction: a restriction that prohibits or limits trade between countries

tundra: a region of treeless plains and permanently frozen soil around the Arctic Circle

tung tree: an Asian tree whose seeds yield a pale yellow oil used in making quick-drying varnishes and waterproofing agents

Index